MY BED

ENCHANTING WAYS TO FALL ASLEEP AROUND THE WORLD

Words by
Rebecca Bond

Pictures by
Salley Mavor

HOUGHTON MIFFLIN HARCOURT | Boston   New York

My bed rocks on the water.

In the Netherlands, some children live on houseboats on canals or rivers. Like everything else in these children's homes, their beds move gently up and down with the waves.

My bed sways in the breeze.

For centuries, sleeping in hammocks has been a tradition in Brazil, Mexico, and other countries of South and Central America. Hammocks provide a comfortable and transportable way of resting, and in some cases also protect against scorpions and snakes.

My bed's beneath a curtain.

In warm, humid parts of the world, such as India, finely woven netting prevents mosquito bites, even when one is sleeping with the windows wide open.

My bed's aloft in trees.

In traditional homes nestled in the mountains of Norway, children sleep nestled into beds that are nestled into walls. These alcove, or cubby, beds save space, offer privacy, and help keep sleepers warm.

My bed's a rug of woven wool my father's mother made.

At night in Afghanistan, many families lay mattresses atop soft, hand-woven rugs and sleep together in a common room. In the morning, they fold their bedding to the side.

My bed's a mat of river grass that lies beneath tree shade.

During the dry season in parts of Ghana, children may prefer to nap outside in the fresh air. Courtyards provide sheltered places to doze on mats or mattresses, which can be brought inside during the night once temperatures turn cooler.

My bed is made from fired clay and heated from below.

In northern parts of the world, such as Russia, winter temperatures can be so cold that many homes have a large stove for cooking and heating. Thick walls make the stove safe to touch and a cozy place to sleep.

My bed unrolls on grasslands vast—it travels where I go.

In the wide-open steppes of Mongolia, nomadic people move when the seasons change to find fresh pastures for their horses, sheep, and yaks, just as their ancestors have for centuries.

My bed is in the courtyard— our family's private space.

Some traditional homes in Iran and other parts of the Middle East are built around a cool, peaceful courtyard. High walls offer a quiet, private outdoor place to rest on hot summer nights.

My bed is on the rooftop – the coolest sleeping place.

In some desert areas of North Africa, including parts of Morocco, scorching summer days give way to cool nights. What better place to catch a dreamy breeze and gaze at the stars than on the roof?

My bed is
built from
sturdy wood.
My bed is warm.
My bed is good.

Many bed frames in Canada and the
United States are made of wood that
comes from these countries' forests.
Hardwoods like maple, walnut, cherry,
oak, and birch make for strong beds that
last for many years and can be passed
down from generation to generation.

My bed's a futon
on the floor.
There is no bed
I could love more.

For hundreds of years, people in Japan have slept on mattresses called futons. A futon sits on the floor atop a straw mat called a tatami. In the morning, children roll up their futons and put them in a closet—or hang them out a window to keep them fresh.

Can you see me
in my bed?
I fit so nicely,
toe to head.

My bed is mine.
And *me*.
And right.
It's bedtime
now for me —

Good night!

To Iris — R.B.

To Rebecca and the children of the world — S.M.

The illustrations in this book were created using fabric, beads,
wire, and yarn on embroidered fabric backgrounds.

The text type was set in Hombre and ITC Legacy Sans Std.
The display type was handstitched by Salley Mavor.

Designed by Whitney Leader-Picone

Library of Congress Cataloging-in-Publication Data
Names: Bond, Rebecca, 1972–2017 author. | Mavor, Salley, illustrator.
Title: My bed / Rebecca Bond ; illustrated by Salley Mavor.
Description: Boston ; New York : Houghton Mifflin Harcourt, [2019]
Identifiers: LCCN 2017024795 |
ISBN 9780544949065
Subjects: LCSH: Beds—Juvenile literature. | Sleeping customs—Juvenile literature.
Classification: LCC GT457 .B66 2019 | DDC 392.3/6—dc23
LC record available at https://lccn.loc.gov/2017024795

Manufactured in China
SCP 10 9 8 7 6 5 4 3 2 1
4500800558

Note About the Stitching

In creating the illustrations for *My Bed*, I feel as if I've gotten to visit all the children in the places they live around the globe, even though I stayed home. Rebecca Bond wrote a narrative that celebrates our differences, while also bringing us together through the universal theme of children sleeping safe in their beds. It was my job to bring these children to life and create their varying environments. When making the artwork for each of the featured locations, I thought about what makes each child's bed and home unique as well as warm and welcoming. Deciding which patterns, details, and traditions to represent wasn't easy. A single country often has many ways of sleeping, and similar traditions are often shared by many countries.

My aim was to portray a distinct sense of place for each culture, using architecture, furnishings, and landscapes as guides. I researched the different regions, looking at photos of children and their living situations, both inside and out, now and in the past. Traditional designs and patterns were of special interest to me as I relish embroidering details at every opportunity. For example, the rug on the Afghanistan page is handstitched with naturally dyed wool yarn, and the cherry blossoms in the tree on the Japan page are stitched with French knots.

In fact, all the original artwork was stitched entirely by hand. I embroidered, wrapped, and bound together a variety of materials with techniques I've developed through years of